PRANAYAMA FOR EVERYONE

PRANAYAMA A LIFE'S FUEL

NAVEEN DESHPETE

ISBN 978-93-5667-151-5
© NAVEEN DESHPETE 2022
Published in India 2022 by Pencil

A brand of

One Point Six Technologies Pvt. Ltd.
123, Building J2, Shram Seva Premises,
Wadala Truck Terminal, Wadala (E)
Mumbai 400037, Maharashtra, INDIA
E connect@thepencilapp.com
W www.thepencilapp.com

DISCLAIMER: *The opinions expressed in this book are those of the authors and do not purport to reflect the views of the Publisher.*

Author biography

I am the founder of breathe studio and pranayama instructor. The book is all about basic pranayama techniques for the busy lifestyle which anyone can easily understand and practice some basic exercises explained with pictures.

Pranayama is crucial in ridding our bodies of many harmful toxins.

CONTENTS

History of Yoga

Before we begin, let's go back to the beginning.

To tell the truth, no one knows!!

Maharshi Patanjali is credited with establishing Yoga as a science.

In the third century B.C., he lived in India.

However, archaeological excavations at Indus Valley civilization sites have revealed

Sculptures and idols depicting various Asanas (physical exercises) discovered

Yoga positions) and these idols date back to around 3000 years B.C.

Vedic texts also contain information on various aspects of Yoga

Such as Shwetashwatrupanishad and Chaandogyopanishad

Upanishad Kaushik, Maitri Upanishad, for example.

This information was dispersed throughout the world, and Maharshi Patanjali compiled it.

INTRODUCTION

The Breathing Science of the Vedas
Pranayama is the most important aspect of Yoga.
Pranayama is made up of two basic Sanskrit words—
Pran= "Life or Universal Life Energy".
Ayam=to extend and lengthen.
Thus, Pranayama is defined as "an exercise to be performed if you want to live a longer life."
Pranayama .
Here's an interesting analogy: You're probably aware of the existence of the seven (7) chakras along the spine, which are thought to be energy points that sustain life and health.
If the Chakras are the rotating windmills that produce energy to sustain life, then prana is the essential wind energy that causes the windmill's hands to rotate in order to produce that energy.
When we breathe in, we take in both the necessary oxygen and the all-pervading Prana.
And when we exhale, we expel the expended energy and toxins from our bodies.]
Ayurveda refers to our digestion as 'Jathar Agni,' which literally means 'digestive fire,' and compares it to a 'Yadnya,' which is a holy pyre where things are offered to the gods.
And the 'Prana' we consume serves as fuel for this holy

Yadnya.

We regulate and streamline the process of drawing in the universal life force when we practice Pranayama, which improves our health and longevity.

This is the Prana metaphysical aspect of it.

Pranayama is crucial in ridding our bodies of these harmful toxins.

It provides an abundant supply of fresh oxygen to our lungs and thus our blood.

It strengthens our immune system.

It is extremely effective at calming your mind.

It aids in memory enhancement, virility, and neurological system strengthening.

There are numerous other Pranayama techniques that can be used for a variety of other purposes.

(Don't worry, I'll tell you everything about those techniques :))

There are seven widely known and practiced Pranayama techniques.

Yet, there are many more techniques (almost 50+ that I came across during my study of Pranayama techniques) which are not easily available to the common public, but have to be actively searched for in various scriptures and Upanishads, which work wonders and are nearly miraculous in their effectiveness. Starting with the most commonly known ones, I have compiled the most effective and beneficial 14 of those breathing techniques in this book for you.

SOME ESSENTIAL TERMINOLOGIES

Here are some terms you'll encounter in this book

Purak- Breathing Terminologies To use your entire lung capacity when inhaling. Also, instead of expanding your stomach, fill all the air in your chest when you inhale.

Kumbhak- ('Kumbh' means a pot or a round utensil) A pot or a round utensil used to hold inhaled air in your lungs.

Rechak— To expel every last ounce of air from your lungs.

Bandh or Lock Terminology-Jalandhar Bandh—closing your windpipe by pressing your chin against the base of your neck.

Uddiyan Bandh—To contract your abdomen and suck in your stomach until it touches your spine.

Mula Bandh is used to tighten the anal muscles. (It's as if you need to use the restroom but can't find one nearby and have to hold it in.

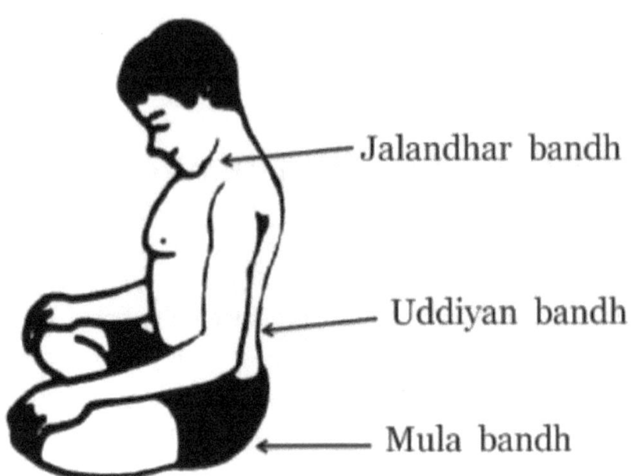

Jalandhar bandh
Uddiyan bandh
Mula bandh

SEATING POSITIONS FOR PRANAYAMA PRACTICE

The majority of the Pranayama should be done while sitting in the 'Sukhasan' position.

Sukhasan (Simple Sitting Pose) – Sit on the mat with your legs stretched out in front of you.

Fold the right leg and pull in underneath the left thigh.
Fold your left leg and pull it between your right thigh and calf.
Sit up straight with your spine erect.

(This is how we sit on the floor and fold our legs.)

10 MOST EFFECTIVE PRANAYAMAS

Pranayama #1

Bhastrika Pranayama/ Bellow Breath

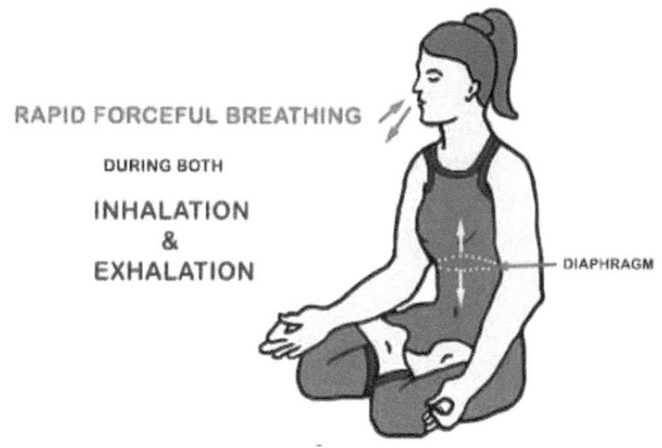

Bhastrika Pranayama
Method: Sit in Sukhasan and form the dyanamudra with your hands on your knees, palms facing upwards.
('Dyanamudra' is formed by joining the tips of your index and middle fingers while keeping your other fingers

outstretched.) Keep your eyes closed.

Inhale completely, hold your breath for a few seconds, and then slowly exhale.

When you inhale, fill your lungs with air and expand your chest, which will press your diaphragm down; do not expand your stomach while inhaling.

Concentrate solely on your breathing and pay close attention to how you feel with each breath.

Consider how each breath nourishes every part of your body.

Duration: Do this Pranayama for 3 minutes.

Uses: -This is a nourishing exercise that improves digestion and generates heat in the body.

It aids in the burning of excess fat.

It aids in the reduction of phlegm.

It is extremely effective in the treatment of Asthma.

It helps to strengthen your lungs.

It aids in blood purification and promotes proper blood circulation.

Pranayama 2 Kapalbhati for cleaning the forehead

Procedure: While in Sukhasan, make the dyanamudra with your hands, place them on your heart, and then your palms facing up, on your knees.

Close your eyes.

After that, quickly exhale in one motion the contraction of your lungs

Your stomach will be sucked in at that time.

Don't intentionally breathe in; after you exhale quickly, breathing in will occur naturally.

Reflex.

Repeat the exhalation motion each time you take a breath in.

Imagine that every impurity, poisonous substance, and unpleasant thought are being expelled from your body.

Caution: - People suffering from back pain and waist pain should perform the exhaling motion a bit slowly. - People suffering with Heart diseases should perform the exhaling motion slowly. - Pregnant women should NOT practice this Pranayama.

Practice this Pranayama for 4-5 minutes at first, and then progressively extend it to 12–15 minutes with consistent practice. (If at first you start to feel fatigued, pause for a short while, and then start again.) Uses:

The advantages of this Pranayama will astound you.

It aids in the burning of extra fat.

It greatly aids in controlling blood sugar levels, which controls diabetes.

It has been discovered to be quite successful in removing heart blockages in those with arteriosclerosis. (However, if you could, exhale slowly.) -It keeps your liver in good shape.

It aids in relieving constipation.

Even better, it has been noted that frequent practice of this Pranayama heals Hepatitis.

It lessens the quantity of phlegm in your body and is also quite beneficial for people with asthma.

It is extremely beneficial for those with dust and pollen allergies.

It has been noted that performing this Pranayama regularly can lessen the growth of cysts and tumors in the body. (There have been numerous instances when patients have reported that frequent, disciplined practice of this Pranayama has caused their tumors to totally disappear.)

It has been discovered to treat all uterine disorders in women.

It has even been discovered to be incredibly efficient at treating skin conditions.

It has a great deal of success in treating throat conditions.

Pranayama 3 Bahya Pranayama Exterior Pranayama

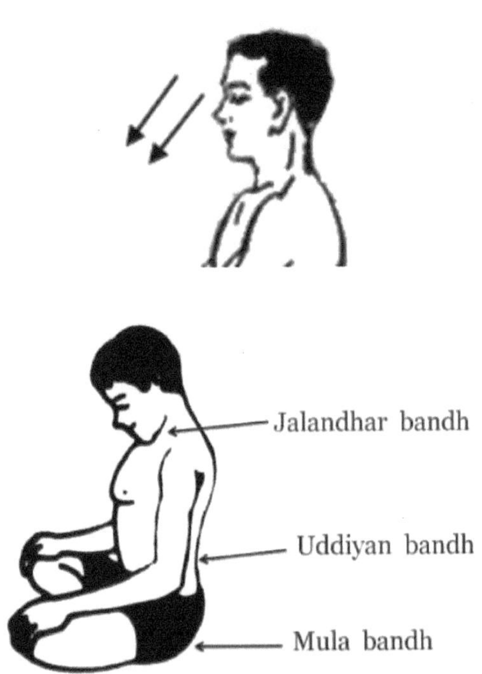

Method: While seated in Sukhasan, make the dyanamudra with your hands and place them palms up on your knees. Close your eyes.

When you exhale, use a little force to try to quickly empty your lungs after taking a deep breath in and holding it for a few seconds.

Implement the next three blocks after you have completely exhaled (you will hear a screaming sound).

Pull your anal muscles in as if you're trying to hold your bowels in while performing the "Muladharbandh" exercise.

Pull in your stomach as if you're trying to touch your stomach to your spine by performing the "Uddiyanbandh" pose.

The "Jalandharbandh" is performed by pressing your chin on your throat while gazing straight down.

Remove all three of the aforementioned blocks for a brief period of time before slowly inhaling to your maximum capacity.

Precaution: People with cardiac conditions shouldn't perform this pranayama.

-People with Spondilitis and Cervical issues shouldn't use the Jalandharbandh (3rd block).

No set time limit, but only do this pranayama three to four times.

Uses:

It helps to make your stomach stronger.

It improves your capacity for digestion.

It is effective in treating hernias.

Your thyroid's health is maintained.

It makes your lungs stronger.

Its most useful use is to enhance the effects of Kapaalbhati Pranayama.

Pranayama 4 Suryabhedan PranayamaPranayama of the Sun

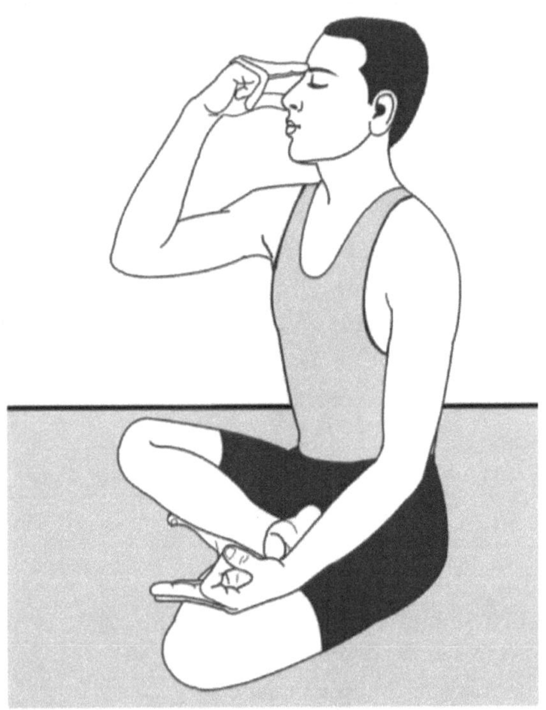

Method: While in Sukhasan, place your left hand, palm down, on your left knee.

Close your eyes.

With the index finger of your right hand, cover your left nostril and take deep breaths through your right nose until you feel full. Once your lungs are full, hold the air in and perform the "Jalandharbandh" [Neck Lock] (press your chin on your throat and look straight down) for as long as you can hold your breath in. (Inhale slightly forcefully so that the air rushing in will produce a sound.)

Remove the neck lock, close your right nostril with the thumb of your right hand, and exhale through your left nostril with enough force to cause your exhalation to produce a sound.

Duration: Do this breathing exercise for no more than 2-3 rounds or repetitions at first. Gradually increase it to 10–12 rounds per session.

Uses:

Regular practice of this Pranayama reduces the amount of cough and phlegm in your body. -It is very helpful in removing toxic gases from your body. -It generates heat within one's body. -It helps in blood purification. -It enhances one's digestive capabilities.

Pranayama 5 Lion Pose (Simhasana)

The English word "lion" is frequently used to translate the Sanskrit word simha, which normally means "mighty one," "hero," or "excellent person."

Preliminary

The Lion-recommended sitting position may be painful to a greater orlesser extent. Leaning forward while pressing your hands to the floor in Thunderbolt Pose, placing your hands and knees in a sort of table position on the ground. (Make sure the belt from the prior exercise is off.) Then slowly recline with your right ankle crossed over your left. Your perineum will settle over and on top of your elevated left heel. Keep in mind that many of these traditional yoga positions include pressing one or both heels against the perineum in order to activate the root foundation wheel (muladhara-chakra) and "block" the torso's bottom exit. Although it is possible to sit with both knees more or less on the floor, typically the knee of the top leg lifts off the floor (while the shin of the bottom leg stays on the floor). With elbows extended, cup one palm over each knee on the same side.

Practice

For a few breaths, breathe normally while loosening the perineum over your heel.

Next, take a deep breath in and hold it for a moment. Although the traditional books instruct you to practice this exercise with Net-Bearer Bond, which involves dropping your chin to or near your sternum, you can omit this step if you like. Now extend your tongue out of your mouth, curling it down toward your chin, and open your mouth as widely as you can while crossing your eyes to look at the middle of your forehead (or the tip of your nose). I once read in the newspaper about researchers discovering a lizard with its tongue embedded in its lower belly. If you were this reptile, you would extend your tongue from its actual base.

Pranayama 6 Bhramari Pranayama step by step guide and its benefits

This breathing exercise activity helps calm the nervous system and produces a relaxing effect on your brain. Brahmari Pranayama is practiced to relieve mental stress, fatigue and vital signs such as body temperature, blood pressure, breathing rate and heart rate. Positively affects ear, nose, mouth and eye problems. This is one of the simplest breathing techniques and can be worked anywhere. There is no need for proper timing to do this pranayama.Preposition• Sitting upright in Dhamasana or in any asana position such as Sukhasana (Sunny and Reverse).• Close your eyes and take a deep breath.• Now put your thumb on your ear and touch it gently.• Place both your index fingers on the top and rest of the fingers on the closed eyelids.• Gently, apply pressure to the side of your nose with the remaining fingertip.• Start breathing air through both nostrils and deeply.• Now, try to focus your mind between the eyebrows.• Close your mouth, exhale, make funny sounds like "hmmm" and "om".• Keep your body calm by feeling positive energy.• Repeat this process 10-11 times.• This can be an excellent meditation technique when you feel stressed and tired.• Remember, when you focus your mind, you are connected to all positive energy in the world, not negative energy.

Benefits of Brahmari Pranayama

Bhramari pranayama is the most effective pranayama for maintaining good health.It helps connect us with our true inner self and keeps us high in positive energy.It is advised and prescribed by homeopaths in almost all health cases for faster recovery. Here is a list of health benefits of Bhramari Pranayama or Bee breathing technique.• Best breathing technique to activate and increase concentration of mind.• Get quick relief from anger, anxiety, stress, insomnia and cerebral tension.• During pregnancy, if you practice Bhramari Pranayama regularly, it facilitates easy and normal child birth.• Vibration from the humming sound stimulates the pineal and pituitary gland to support normal functions.• It is the best treatment to treat Alzheimer's disease.• It helps reduce migraine pain.• By practicing this technique we can control our thoughts and the mind becomes steady with positive energy.

Best time to practice Bhramari Pranayama:• Bhramari Pranayama is best practiced on an empty stomach between 4 AM and 6 AM. Although it can be practiced at any time of the day, Bhramari (like most pranayama) is terribly powerful in predominantly silent spaces with few distracting sounds. Our inner perception is more acute in silence and fresh air.

Precautions for Bhramari Pranayama• Do not practice in a relaxed back position or supine position.• Do not press too hard on the ear and eye cartilage. Gently press with fingers and release.• Do not put your finger inside your ear.• This bee breathing technique should be done on an empty stomach.• Consult your doctor if you suffer from rhinorrhea or ear infection before doing Bhramari Pranayama.• There is no exact time to perform this technique but if you practice it early in the morning around sunrise this asana can do wonders for your health.• Do not hold breath for long if you are pregnant and have heart disease.• Mental stress is one of the major problems especially among students who have exam stress and study stress. People in metros also face the same problems due to high work pressure and heavy traffic. Pranayama is the best way to connect the soul with God, because you hold the air that God is with you while letting go rather than approaching God. Bhramari is a pranayama commonly known as humming bee breath technique which can be done anywhere to reduce mental stress, depression, anxiety, frustration and anger or at the same time it soothes our nervous system very well. Bhramari Pranayama works more in predominantly silent places where you connect your mind to your soul effectively.

Pranayama 7 Sama Vritti Pranayama (Equal Breathing)

Many yogis consider breathing to be a powerful and essential part of one's yoga practice. When a yogi can control his breath, he can control his prana or life force energy, which controls everything he thinks, feels and does. One of the best breathing techniques you can use to create a calm and peaceful mind is Sama Vritti Pranayama. It is a simple yet highly effective yoga breathing exercise that can be practiced by anyone at any time. Mastering this technique will help you focus your mind to improve your meditation and yoga. Practicing this breath creates a foundation for learning more advanced pranayamasWhat is Sama Vritti Pranayama?Sama Vritti Pranayama is a yogic breathing exercise also known as Sama Vrittis or box breathing. Sama means "equal", and vritti means "mental fluctuations", so Sama vritti pranayama translates to "breathing of equal mental fluctuations". Samavrti Pranayama is a proportional breathing technique that uses a set length of equal inhalations, exhalations and breath holds. The main goal of this technique is to reduce mental chatter and confusion.

Benefits of Sama Vritti Pranayama

The main benefit of this pranayama practice is to equalize, harmonize and balance the prana flowing through the nadis or energy channels of the body. This four-part breathing technique is primarily practiced to calm and balance the mind and body to reduce mental stress and worry. Conscious use of the diaphragm to increase air flow to the lungs is a great way to improve your ability to breathe deeply and bring oxygen to the lungs. Sama Vrittis helps to slow the heart rate, increase oxygen to the brain and reduce anxiety. People who regularly practice this yoga breathing technique are more focused and able to experience deep, restful relaxation.How to practice: Step-by-step instructions

Practicing Equal Breathing Find your seat - Find a

comfortable cross-legged sitting position on the floor, straightening the back of the body. Place the backs of your hands on your legs, touching the tips of the index fingers and thumbs (Jnana Mudra). Make sure you don't have tension in your body and take special care to relax the shoulders. If you are not comfortable on the floor, a chair can be used but make sure the feet rest flat on the floor and the back is straight. You can practice this lying on your back, perhaps with your legs on a bolster and the knees slightly elevated.

Find your breath - close your mouth, inhale and exhale through the nose in a slow and continuous flow. Use diaphragmatic breathing so that the belly rises and falls with little or no movement in the chest.Adjust your pace – Slow down and make your breathing comfortable. Most importantly, breathe in and out of the body at your own pace. If you start to struggle, then reduce the length and number of counts.Begin your breathing cycle• Breathe out for a count of 4.• Hold the breath for a count of 4.• Exhale for a count of 4.• Hold the breath for a count of 4.Find your flow - repeat the four-part cycle of breathing for another 2-6 rounds. As you become comfortable with the practice, you can increase the duration to 10-30 breaths or a maximum of 10 minutes. Continue only as long as you are present and focused with the breathing practice.Practice tipsFor a more advanced version, add Ujjai breathing to your technique. This adds a warming effect and helps block out external noise.To make this breathing exercise more intense and challenging, you can increase the length of the count to 6.If you find that you are struggling with breathing, reduce and decrease the count to 2 or 3 until it feels easier. You can eliminate breath holding and the cycle of breathing with just inhalations and exhalations.Daily pranayama practice is recommended to quickly learn this technique and reap its many benefits.Most importantly, do not switch to unevenly proportioned breathing, as this affects the quality and benefits of pranayama practice. If you can't maintain an even ration, it's best to stop, rest for a few breaths, and then try again.

When to use Sama Vritti Pranayama

Sama Vritti Pranayama can be practiced at any time of the day, but the best time to practice is when you need to develop inner peace, balance and grounding. Ideally find a quiet place away from distractions so you can fully focus and tune into your breath. Yoga is recommended to be practiced before other practices as it helps prepare the body and mind for asana practice, meditation and other forms of pranayama. You can use this technique while holding yoga poses to increase your concentration.

Pranayama 8 Nadi Sodhana Pranayama

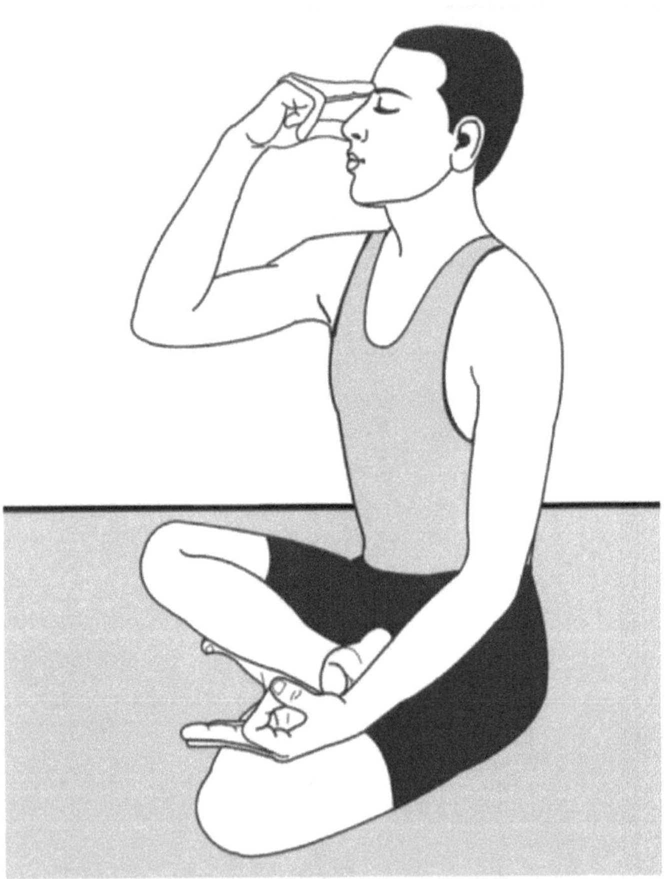

Alternate nostril breathingAlternate nostril breathing is balancing, calming, anti-anxiety and very relaxing.Place the right hand in the Vishnu Mudra (index and middle fingers bent towards the palm; thumb, ring and pinky in the air). To make a round: close the right nostril with the thumb and breathe into the left nostril; Close the left nostril with the ring and pinky fingers, open the right nostril and exhale through the right side, then inhale through the right nostril; Close the right nostril, open the left and exhale through the left nostril. Continue doing 5-20 rounds.

Pranayama 9 Udgeet Pranayama Benefits and Technique

What is Udgeet Pranayama?

The word Udgeet means "deep and rhythmic chanting" while Pranayama means 'breathing exercises' or "mastery of breath and energy". Udgeet Pranayama is a breathing exercise using the rhythmic chanting of the Om mantra. It is derived from the word "Udgita" described in Chandogya Upanishad, one of the oldest yogic scriptures. This scripture defines Udgita as the chanting of the Om mantra. It describes the deep rhythmic chanting of the word Om with conscious control of the breath as the most powerful way to use the mantra.

Benefits of Udgeet Pranayama

Udgeet Pranayama has numerous physical and spiritual benefits. Practicing this pranayama helps strengthen concentration and focus, especially when there are external sounds to distract you. It helps clear negative thoughts and emotions like guilt, fear, anger and sadness. A recent medical study has shown that this breathing practice promotes weight loss and strengthens the lungs by improving lung function. Another study found that chanting Om for 10 minutes improved focus, created a positive mood, and fostered a sense of social cohesion. It helps reduce stress, improve breathing, promote restful sleep and increase energy levels. Spiritually, Udgeet Pranayama can bring about a trance-like state of awareness and create a sense of unity between us and the universe.

Udgeet Pranayama Instructions

Here are the six steps involved in chanting breathing. You can practice this pranayama for 2-10 minutes, 1-2 times a day.Sit in a stable and comfortable position with your spine straight and long. If sitting on the floor, you can use a cushion or folded blanket behind the hips for support. If sitting on a chair, make sure both feet are flat on the floor.Close your eyes or soften your gaze and start taking deep breaths through your nose. Allow your body to relax and bring your awareness to your breath. Make sure there is no strain on the shoulders, neck or face.Focus on using diaphragmatic breathing so that only the belly rises and falls with the breath. Begin chanting the mantra Om with each exhalation.Work on holding the breaths for as long as possible without tiring. Allow the breath to create the sound.Concentrate on the vibration of the voice and the sensation of the breath as you chant Om. Experiment with sound loud enough to focus your attention on the practice.Repeat the chant while slowing your breathing and focusing your attention. End the practice with a moment of silence to integrate your experience.

Breathing Practice Tips

Breathing exercises should always be done in moderation and without strain. If you feel tired or dizzy, stop and rest.When practicing any form of breathing, it is best to start small and gradually increase the amount of time practiced each week.It is recommended not to force yourself to breathe deeply if you are feeling anxious or stressed. Instead, focus on relaxing your mind and body before starting your session.Deep breathing techniques can help reduce stress levels and anxiety, but they are not a substitute for therapy or medication.If you have a medical condition, it is best to consult your doctor before starting any type of yoga or breathing exercises.

Pranayama 10 Sit Kari Pranayama

A deep breath cools the body and calms the mind.Roll the tongue touching the roof of the mouth as far back as you can for a soft palette. As you inhale, clench your teeth together and part your lips slightly to make a "ssss" sound. Exhale through both nostrils. Repeat 5-10 times.

Contradiction
Use this pranayama only if there is obvious excess heat in the body. Do not use if the body is cold and practice with caution in winter.

www.ingramcontent.com/pod-product-compliance
Lightning Source LLC
LaVergne TN
LVHW041444170726
843492LV00008B/2793